Helping Your Family Grieve

Lament and Remember Together

Darby A. Strickland

New Growth Press

newgrowthpress.com

New Growth Press, Greensboro, NC 27401
newgrowthpress.com
Copyright © 2024 by Darby A. Strickland

Cover Design: Dan Stelzer
Interior Typesetting/eBook: Lisa Parnell, lparnellbookservices.com

ISBN 978-1-64507-460-1 (Print)
ISBN 978-1-64507-461-8 (eBook)

Library of Congress Cataloging-in-Publication Data
Names: Strickland, Darby A., author.
Title: Helping your family grieve : walking with Jesus in heartbreak / Darby A. Strickland.
Description: Greensboro, NC : New Growth Press, [2024]
Identifiers: LCCN 2024001975 (print) | LCCN 2024001976 (ebook) | ISBN
    9781645074601 (print) | ISBN 9781645074618 (ebook)
Subjects: LCSH: Grief--Religious aspects--Christianity. | Bereavement--Religious aspects--Christianity. | Consolation.
Classification: LCC BV4905.3 .S77 2024 (print) | LCC BV4905.3 (ebook) |
    DDC 248.8/66--dc23/eng/20240222
LC record available at https://lccn.loc.gov/2024001975
LC ebook record available at https://lccn.loc.gov/2024001976

Printed in India

29 28 27 26 25   4 5 6 7 8

We grieve because we have lost someone precious to us. Someone we love deeply; someone we miss; someone who is irreplaceable. The grief that surrounds death is pervasive and profound. It does not easily relent, and it cannot be avoided. But do not let that be a discouragement to you. We grieve because we love. And that love should be cherished.

When your family loses someone precious to all of you, all of you grieve together. This is a hard place to be. In the days ahead, you will be grieving and your children will also be struggling with the death of someone they love. This is painful. But keep sight of the fact that there is something precious about loving someone. Our love for people does not die with them. It lives on. It just takes time for that love to be a source of joy; presently, it is a source of great loss and pain.

Loss overwhelms and children do not know how to respond to it. Their hearts burst with big emotions and lots of questions. They will need your help to express the sadness, fear, and anger that come after encountering the realities of death. Here's the good news: God has given us a pathway through grief. Though it likely feels impossible to go forward today, our God promises to lead us up and out of the dark valleys of our lives (Psalm 23). Your children need you to walk with them on the pathway through grief.

This might seem impossible to do as you also navigate the hard road of grief. Someone you cherished is gone. Their death has ushered in a season of unwelcome change. Grief overwhelms, even destabilizes. You probably feel a deep sadness and emotional exhaustion. Your grief comes in waves. Some days are harder than others. Grief is also highly personal. No one really knows how your loss affects you. It has an isolating quality about it. Consequently, it is more difficult to connect with others. With such complex suffering, it is hard to have hope, let alone hold out comfort and hope for your children.

This booklet will guide you and your children through these challenges. It will give you two orienting directions to help you navigate an unwanted grief journey. The first is to help you and your children speak directly to the Lord about your sadness and look for his comfort. The second is to give your family opportunities to remember your loved one, which will encourage healing and connection. But before we get to how you can help your children, let's prioritize processing your grief.

Tend to Your Own Sorrow

Our children watch us so they can make sense of their world, and in doing so, they learn to respond to it. Whether we realize it or not, much of what we teach is through modeling. When my children were young, I learned that I expressed frustration with heavy sighs because I watched my toddlers mimic me in their frustration. It was a convicting mirror! I learned quickly where I needed to grow. But they also picked up on my husband's quickness to pray when overwhelmed. When they saw me stretched by the day's demands, they said, "Mommy, it looks like you need to ask God for help." Children learn more by watching us than they learn from our words.

The same is true of grief. Our examples teach our children. A large part of shepherding your children through grief is to model how to bring your loss and sadness to the Lord. Yet many of us do not know how to grieve, or it hasn't been modeled for us. This means we have to learn to grieve by faith if we want to help our children heal. Please recognize this as a gift from the Lord. He does not want you to deny the difficulties or hide your sadness and tears. God wants to tend to your sorrow. Our Lord is faithful. He promises to be with us in our suffering and give us the grace we need to endure (Deuteronomy 31:8). As you seek the Lord's comfort, he will grant it.

So what does it look like for Christian parents to lead their children through grief? We often hear about people "being strong" and receiving praise for keeping difficult emotions and tears to themselves. But this is not how God tells us to grieve. The Psalms show us that God welcomes expressions of sorrow. He wants us to bring him our whole hearts. We even see Jesus crying over his friend Lazarus's death and meeting Mary and Martha in their distress over the loss of their brother (John 11). Scripture also tells us we should seek support from God and our community during hardships (James 5:13–18), and it instructs us to carry one another's burdens (Galatians 6:2). Our need for God's help is great in seasons of loss. As we learn to depend upon him and his people, so do our children.

When God provides us comfort, it benefits our children. As your children watch you seeking comfort and help from him and others, they learn about God's faithfulness and presence in times of trouble. Our children learn where to place their hope as we cling to the promise that "the LORD is near to the brokenhearted and saves the crushed in spirit" (Psalm 34:18). But as God comforts us, he also gifts us the ability to help our children. Scripture tells us that as we receive comfort, we will be able to comfort others with the same comfort we have received (2 Corinthians 1:3–6).

May this encourage you to take every opportunity to pray and ask others to pray for you. Ask for God's Spirit to bring you peace that only he can grant, encouragement through his Word, friends who shoulder burdens, and strength for the day ahead.

Your children need you to prioritize tending to your grief so that you can care for them.

Eventually, your children will see you experiencing peace amid sorrow, receiving strength from prayers, clinging to God's promises, having courage for difficult moments, and being gifted with friends who help when you are overwhelmed.

Understand Your Children's Grief

The ages of your children will largely determine how they express and process grief. Toddlers and preschoolers will struggle to understand the permanence of the loss. As a result, they might repeatedly ask for the person who died. Younger children lack the language and concepts to process emotions, but they will still experience all the unsettling emotions that accompany grief.

Grieving children face two major emotions: instability and despair. Since developmentally they cannot yet reason through language, be on the lookout for how their grief shows up through behavior. A child's grief might manifest itself in struggles with sleep, nightmares, separation anxiety, developmental regressions (e.g., relapses in potty training, talking like a baby, etc.), displays of anger, themes of death showing up in their play and drawings, and having emotional outbursts.

In their attempt to understand what has happened, children will ask lots of questions about death. They might ask if you and they will die too.

It is important that you answer their questions honestly but in a way that is filled with the hope of the gospel and the promise of God's care. Your instinct might be to protect your children by shielding them from hard realities, but your children need you to be their trusted guide. Age-appropriate honesty is key to fostering trust and reliability.

Though you and your children grieve differently, you can move through loss together—each of you can turn to the Lord in your suffering. As you practice turning to the Lord, you will show your children how to do this as well.

The grieving process is not something to be rushed. It requires a willingness to sit in a place of suffering. But you do not sit there alone. Your Savior is with you. He promises, "I will never leave you nor forsake you" (Hebrews 13:5). He is "a man of sorrows" (Isaiah 53:3). He understands your pain, loss, and fears. He invites you to speak to him about your grief and heartache because he wants to accompany you on your grief journey. He desires to walk alongside you, to uphold and uplift you.

Lament through Loss

One way God stays close in our grief is by meeting us when we lament. Lament is a prayer where we pour out our sorrows with a purpose—building trust. When we express our sufferings, heartaches, confusions, and fears directly to the Lord, it renews our confidence in our Comforter.

Telling the Lord about our distress is important to him, so he gives us many examples of this in his Word. Many psalms are cries of lament (6, 10, 13, 25, 42, 43, 130), and then of course there is the book of Lamentations. These writings encourage us to speak directly to God with tear-filled eyes. We can ask him for help by borrowing their words.

We even see our Savior's distress on the cross. He cries out to God using psalms. Jesus tells God he feels both abandoned by him (Psalm 22:1) and willing to trust him amid his anguish (Psalm 31:5). God wants us to use his words when it is hard to find our own because they point us to his comfort.

We can come to God with our raw emotions. Consider these cries from Psalm 6:6: "I am weary with my moaning; every night I flood my bed with tears; I drench my couch with my weeping." Speaking to God about your distress might make you uncomfortable, especially if you wrestle with how God cares for you. But do not let that stop you. God already knows how your heart is struggling and invites you to talk to him about it. He will not be offended.

Scripture even gives us ways to speak to him about feeling abandoned by him. Listen as King David laments: "I am weary with my crying out; my throat is parched. My eyes grow dim with waiting for my God" (Psalm 69:3). There is no trouble in our heart that we cannot bring to him. Rest assured: he will answer you, just like he reminded David that his love is a redeeming love that seeks to restore what is broken (Psalm 138). He will remind you of his faithfulness to you as well.

To heal, we need to process our pain and possess hope; lamenting helps us do both. Psalms not only give us words of sorrow to speak but also gently remind us of God's love, presence, protection, and care. Psalm 10:17 says, "O Lord, you hear the desire of the afflicted; you will strengthen their heart; you will incline your ear."

God promises that our Good Shepherd will never leave us and will one day take us to heaven to be with him. In Psalm 23, we learn that his people "shall dwell in the house of the Lord forever" (v. 6). Jesus spells this out for us even further: "In my Father's house are many rooms. . . . [I]f I go and prepare a place for you, I will come again and will take you to myself, that where I am you may be also" (John 14:2–3). His good words guide us in our grief and help us guide our children. He tells us that those who love him will be with him. This can also give us hope of reuniting with our loved ones one day.

Are you starting to see how important lament is? Lament allows us to find hope and healing amid the instability and despair accompanying loss. It does not rush you through your sadness; it embraces and anticipates it.

Children also need ways to speak about their pain, and they need us to help them find the words. What better words can we give them than God's words? To care for your children in loss, you will need to teach them how to lament.

Teach Your Children to Lament

To begin caring for your children in loss, you will need to provide space and permission for them to grieve and lament. This means slowing down their emotions when they rise to the surface and drawing them out in conversation.

Because it is hard to watch our children suffer, we often want to move them through their pain quickly. Sometimes we try to distract or redirect them when they are sad because we do not like to see them in pain. But grief should not be passed by. Instead, sit with them while they weep, allow their sadness to linger, and encourage them to talk about it. You will probably need to help them identify what they are feeling. Tell them it's okay to feel sad. Ask them if they are feeling scared, mad, or confused.

Scripture tells us to weep with those who weep; it is one way we are called to love (Romans 12:15). It is good to cry with your children and cry out to the Lord together. Do not be afraid that your children are not healing if they are sad. Expressing their sadness helps them to heal. Ask God for the strength to watch them grieve as you rely on Jesus's promise to comfort those who mourn (Matthew 5:4). When we entrust our children to the Lord's faithful care and comforting presence (Isaiah 43:2), we will gain the strength to watch them grieve.

As you hear your children's distress, you help them shape it into a lament. Similar to grief, this process takes time. Even as we consider the Psalms as our guide, the struggles and promises they capture often take months, if not years, to sort through. Many laments captured by a psalm were not written or experienced in just one day; they are the outworking of a long season of struggle and sorrow. The same will be true for your children. So give them many opportunities to share their heart with you and God over time. Remember, when children try to work something out in their young minds, they ask many questions! When they learn a new skill, we witness them practicing it repetitiously. Their experience with grief will be no different.

Lamenting takes faith, and it builds faith. Faith is something we and the Lord are building into our children. Laments are made up of three parts:

1. Talking to God about how you feel.
2. Asking God for help.

3. Remembering God is someone we can place our trust and hope in.

We do not have to talk about all these things in one conversation with our children. In the early days, your children might only be able to talk to God about their feelings or where they need help. Or maybe your children need you to talk to God for them. They might not know how to pray about such deep hurts, so let them listen to you bring their concerns to God. Remember, a lament is something that is built over time. It's a way of interacting with God that takes practice.

Initially, you and your children might struggle to connect your complaints to God's faithfulness. But keep talking to God and reading his Word. He will, in time, help you connect your children's needs to his steadfast love. At the end of this section, I have provided a list of verses that will help you locate tender truths for times of loss. After practicing speaking about suffering as laments, you and your children will be able to move through these three parts more readily in moments of distress. Keep in mind that each piece will foster a child's faith, but they work together to help sufferers gain confidence in God's trustworthiness.

Here are ways you can help your children build a lament.

Talk about how your children feel

Your children might struggle to find the words to describe their feelings, so ask them if they're feeling mad, sad, confused, lonely, afraid, in shock, left behind, helpless, or hurt. Depending on your children's ages, you might ask them to describe what these emotions feel like. You might have to explain, "Loneliness feels like you are all alone, even when there are people around, or it might feel like you are empty inside." Explain that all these are normal feelings of grief.

Remember that a child might wrestle with different emotions each day, so keep asking how they are feeling. Since children lack an advanced vocabulary, they often express their feelings through their behavior (often misbehavior), so keep asking yourself, *What does my children's behavior indicate about what they are feeling and how they are doing?* Try to help them find words for what they are feeling.

Here is a list of emotions that typically accompany grief: anger, confusion, abandonment, insecurity, sadness, loneliness, shock, disbelief, depression, fear, helplessness, relief (if the suffering period was prolonged), tension, guilt, jealousy, emptiness, hopelessness, and fear. I share this list so you can have an idea of what your children might experience and also know that a broad range of challenging emotions is an expected aspect of grief.

Once you have a good understanding of how their heart is doing, give them words to pray. You could say, "God likes it when you tell him how you are doing. Why don't you tell God you feel lonely?" You might need to help them by modeling how to talk to God about your emotions or by praying for them. Use simple language and short sentences.

Ask God for help

God delights in helping his people. In fact, he promises that he is an ever-present help in times of trouble (Psalm 46:1). Share with your children that our God answers prayer. Maybe even tell a story about how he has answered your prayers.

Ask them how they think God can help them. If your children need help knowing what to ask God for, brainstorm with them. If they are sad, lead them to ask for God's comfort (2 Thessalonians 2:16–17). If they are afraid, they can ask God to protect them (Psalm 46:1). When your children feel mad, encourage them to talk to you and God (Psalm 130:1). When they feel alone and do not know what to do, they can ask for God's guidance (Proverbs 3:5–6). Help them ask God for peace when they feel confused (Philippians 4:6–7).

It might be helpful to make a list or pictures of things they can ask God for so they have a visual reference. God's help can feel abstract for children.

One of the best ways to overcome this is to tell them when you see God helping them or others. When friends send an encouraging card or bring over a meal, help your children see that those provisions are from God.

Remember God is someone we can place our trust and hope in

God's greatest act of love was destroying death through the death and resurrection of his Son, Jesus. We have great hope because one day, there will be no more sadness and we will be reunited with those we love in the presence of Jesus. But there are many more biblical promises of God's steadfast love for his people that will comfort us for the days ahead. Just like us, our children must be reminded that the Lord is for us. Almost all the psalms of lament end with an expression of trust, hope, or praise, and so should our prayers.

Here are some tender comforts for times of loss:

- "Blessed are those who mourn, for they shall be comforted" (Matthew 5:4).
- "He heals the brokenhearted and binds up their wounds" (Psalm 147:3).
- "For God so loved the world, that he gave his only Son, that whoever believes in him should not perish but have eternal life" (John 3:16).

- "You will be sorrowful, but your sorrow will turn into joy" (John 16:20b).
- "The Lord is near to the brokenhearted and saves the crushed in spirit" (Psalm 34:18).
- "I lift up my eyes to the hills. From where does my help come? My help comes from the Lord, who made heaven and earth" (Psalm 121:1–2).
- "It is the Lord who goes before you. He will be with you; he will not leave you or forsake you. Do not fear or be dismayed" (Deuteronomy 31:8).
- "He will wipe away every tear from their eyes, and death shall be no more, neither shall there be mourning, nor crying, nor pain anymore, for the former things have passed away" (Revelation 21:4).

Since children benefit from repetition, do not feel you have to come up with something new for each conversation. Repeating the same deep truths is beneficial for them. You can post these verses in your kitchen, in your child's bedroom, on a mirror—anywhere your child can see them in seasons of sorrow and be reminded of God's love for them. In time, you can even help them write out a psalm of their own. Give them words they can remember in their moment of need.

Here is what a child's lament might sound like, based on Psalm 43:

God, help me. Keep me from trouble.
You are my strength! But I feel weak and
     worried.
Why am I so sad?
Remind me that you are a faithful friend,
walking with me in my sadness.
One day, you will lead me out of my sadness.
But today, I am still so sad.
Help me. Help me know you are my helper.
And remind me that you have promised to
     always care for me.

When you teach your children to lament, you learn how they are doing and how they are making sense of what happened. But most importantly, you are teaching them how God fits into their story and how to turn to him in times of great sadness. This is one way you are called to tend to their grief. Another is to help them navigate the impact of the loss, and we do that by helping them remember their loved ones.

Remember a Loved One

While the intensity of the loss diminishes over time, the significance of the person who died determines how long your children will experience its impact. If your children lose a parent or sibling, they will likely experience grief throughout their lives. Not only will they grieve on the anniversary of the loss, but they will also notice the person's absence at key life events and feel the loss differently during various life stages. As time passes, other people will overlook your children's grief. But your children will still need to talk about their loss, and they will need help in knowing how to process grief in different seasons. Sharing memories and creating mementos can help them prepare for and navigate these grief waves as they arise.

Children also might fear they will forget their loved ones, so helping them maintain those memories will comfort them in their grief. They will feel freer to let go of the sadness if they know they can remember the love they shared with the person who is gone. If the loss occurred while a child was young, they might not have many memories. These children often grieve for a relationship that they missed out on having. Sharing memories of a loved one is a great way to recognize these complex feelings.

Remembering is one way we allow space for grief. So do not fear bringing up a lost loved one. We want to give our children the opportunity to experience any feelings they have about the loss and speak about someone they love. As children grow up and experience milestones (e.g., birthdays, graduations, weddings), their loved one's absence will be uniquely felt. Help children find creative ways to include a remembrance of their missing loved one and provide them opportunities to talk about how they are feeling about the loss.

Remembering a loss while continuing to live is vital to healing. God wants your children to continue to experience the joys of life and all the milestones and excitement they have ahead of them. This does not mean moving on from the loss; it means wisely taking it with them. When there has been a significant loss, children greatly benefit when they can move into their new normal, bringing memories of their loved ones with them.

In Scripture, God tells his people in times of trouble to remember his faithfulness to them. He often reminds his people that he is the one who brought them out of slavery. To remind them of his faithfulness, he recalls their suffering. When a child remembers their loved one, you can also help them remember God's care for them in their loss.

Ideas for Remembering a Loved One

One of your most important jobs is to help your children remember the person they lost. Because of your closeness to your children, you will have witnessed or shared many of these memories with them. Remembering for your children these precious moments or unique qualities about their loved one is a gift to them.

There are so many creative ways you can foster remembering. You might prepare some of these ideas now to share with the children when they are older. Other items on this list are activities that can be repeated. It is good to recount positive memories, but do not hesitate to acknowledge the difficult ones.

- Keep a memory box. Collect items that remind you of your loved one—letters, mementos, recipes, small gifts, their favorite verse or Bible, and pictures.
- Plant something in your garden that reminds you of them—their favorite tree or plants that display their favorite colors.
- Write down stories about your loved one.
- Wear something special, perhaps a piece of jewelry or clothing that reminds you of them.
- Share your loved one's story with others.
- Make their favorite meal or go out to their favorite restaurant.
- Turn their favorite T-shirt into a comfy pillow or blanket. Or repurpose clothing into pieces of art, jewelry, or a quilt.
- Make a photobook.
- Hang their favorite Bible verse on the wall.
- Sing their favorite song or hymn.
- Read a book they loved.
- Spend time learning a hobby of theirs.

- Purchase or make a Christmas ornament in their honor.
- Ask others to share stories and record their recollections.
- Visit their favorite place.
- Paint pictures of their favorite things on garden rocks.
- Make a playlist of their favorite songs.
- Watch their favorite movie.
- Donate to or serve a charity they invested in.
- Plan a special activity on their birthday and the anniversary of their death. Share pictures and remember fun you might have had together.
- Spend time with their friends and family.

We gain comfort and strength as we remember someone we love. But sharing memories is also a way to delight in the gift of someone's love and recall what God has done. Consider going through the book *Something Sad Happened* with your children.[1] The story of the bluebird Sunny who is grieving for Wren can be a starting point for talking to your children about grief and pointing them toward lamenting and remembering.

Grief is a journey that doesn't come with linear directions. But it has a destination. God invites us to come to him. We grieve best when we grieve with God. I hope that as you guide your children through grief you will all draw closer to the Lord. Psalm 91 paints the picture of the Lord holding us close, tucking us gently under his wings (v. 4). In times of grief, we remember the Lord is a tender comforter for his people.

Endnote

1. Darby A. Strickland, *Something Sad Happened* (Greensboro, NC: New Growth Press, 2024).

ccef

CCEF is committed to restoring Christ to counseling and counseling to the church. They seek to accomplish this mission through resources, courses, events, and counseling.

To learn more or explore CCEF's resources, visit **ccef.org**.